I0114783

Freedom of Speech
v
Protection of Reputation

Public Interest Defence in American and
English Law of Defamation

Published by
Adonis & Abbey Publishers Ltd
P. O. Box 43418
London
SE11 4XZ
http://www.adonis-abbey.com
Email: editor@adonis-abbey.com

First Edition, January 2010

Copyright 2010 © Jideofor Adibe

British Library Cataloguing-in-Publication Data
A catalogue record for this book is available from the British Library

ISBN:9781906704322

The moral right of the author has been asserted

All rights reserved. No part of this book may be reproduced,
stored in a retrieval system or transmitted at any time or by any
means without the prior permission of the publisher

Layout Artist/Technical Editor, Jan B. Mwesigwa

Freedom of Speech
v
Protection of Reputation

Public Interest Defence in American and
English Law of Defamation

By

Jideofor Adibe

Adonis & Abbey
Publishers Ltd

CONTENTS

TABLE OF CASES

GENERAL INTRODUCTION

Free speech is increasingly recognised as a universal human value, even though its application differs in different jurisdictions. Free speech is however never absolute, even in jurisdictions like the USA, where the First and Fourteenth Amendments give it special protection. The main reason why free speech cannot be absolute is because it competes with other equally important human values such as the right to privacy, reputation or to protect societies from potential harms from unrestrained hate or obscene speech.

In this study we look at how free speech interests are balanced against the need to protect reputation in American and English defamation laws. We studied cases from both countries to see how this tension is resolved. We pay special attention to 'public interest' defence since the media often justifies its attack on reputation on 'public interest', even when it is substituting its own interest for this 'public interest'.

The premise of the study is that while freedom of the press is desirable and cherishable, it is important that the individual is recognised as the foundational block of human rights and the democratic process, who is entitled to his reputation as part of his human dignity. If the notion of human rights is necessarily anti-majoritarian in principle, it means that cases in which the press uses public interest defence to attack reputations require close analyses to ensure that both the individual and the public good are equally protected.

We examined four cases in the US - *New York Times v Sullivan* (involving a public official), *Curtis Publishing Co. v. Butts* (involving a public figure), *Time Inc v Hill* (involving a private individual who was transformed into a public figure against his will), *and Monitor Patriot v Roy* (involving a candidate for a political office). In the UK we examined *Derbyshire County Council v Times Newspapers Ltd. and Others* (involving a local authority, which sued for libel), *Reynolds v Times Newspapers Ltd* (involving a politician), *and George Galloway v Telegraph Group Ltd* (involving a controversial politician who was famous for opposing the Iraq war and the UN's sanctions against the country – both supported by the defendant newspaper). In all these cases, 'public interest' figured prominently as one of the defences by the accused media house. But what is the notion of 'public interest' espoused in the judgment in these cases? And does it sufficiently protect both the public good and the individual?

This work was originally submitted as a dissertation for the Master of Laws (LLM) degree in Media Law at City University, London, and was scored an 'A'. I am gratefully to my supervisor, Professor Ian Loveland, for encouragements, and colleagues at the programme for their various inputs. Obviously any errors of interpretation in the work are mine and are regretted.

Chapter 1

MEANING OF FREE SPEECH AND ITS RATIONALE

Introduction

Generally speaking free speech means the ability of people to speak their mind without censorship. It is recognised as a universal human value, even though it is applied differently in different jurisdictions[1]. Freedom of expression, a broader concept than freedom of speech, is sometimes used as a synonym not just for freedom of verbal speech but also for any act of seeking, receiving and imparting information or ideas, irrespective of the medium used. Free speech is however never absolute in any jurisdiction, primarily because free speech competes with equally important values such as the right to privacy, the protection of people's reputation or the need to protect the society's from potential harms from unrestrained hate or obscene speech.

There are a number of political, philosophical and moral arguments why free speech deserves special protection. In general four arguments are usually put forward to justify a free speech principle:

1) The importance of discovering the truth.

1

2) Free speech as an aspect of self-fulfil-
ment.
3) Free speech as being indispensable for a
citizen to participate in a democracy.
4) There is a strong reason to be suspicious
of governments.[2]

With the increasing globalisation of democracy, public concern in many jurisdictions is no
longer whether free speech should be protected
at all but rather with the scope of the freedom
of speech and how it should be balanced
against other competing values in the society.
Quite often, arguments derived from political
theories play central roles in the disposition of
free speech cases by courts, especially when
the courts have to determine the meaning of
speech or the scope of freedom[3].

Attempts to suppress free speech could
heighten the suspicion of authority and could
also destroy tolerance or drive underground the
suppressed speech, which many could have
otherwise ignored if such had not been suppressed. Suppressing free speech is also contrary to the 'marketplace of ideas' theory
popularised in the dissenting judgment of
Holmes J in *Abrams v US* when he declared:

> But when men have realised that time has upset
> many fighting faiths, they may come to believe
> even more than they believe the very founda-
> tion of their own conduct that the ultimate good
> desired is better reached by free trade in ideas –

that the best test of truth is the power of the
thought to get itself accepted in the competition
of the market, and that truth is the only ground
upon which their wishes safely can be carried
out.[4]

Holmes seemed to have borrowed from the
argument of liberal economists, which posit
that interference with the operation of free
market in goods and services leads to distor-
tions and undermines efficiency. With respect
to free speech, it is recognised that while the
market place of ideas would be very efficient
in promoting the goals of free speech, this
'market' could not be unfettered, because free
speech must be balanced against other competing values in the society. Professor Eugene
Volokh has called this balancing act in many
societies the 'constitutional tension method'.[5]

**Freedom of Speech in English Jurispru-
dence**

In English Common law, prior to the
incorporation of the European Convention on
Human Rights (ECHR) into the UK law by the
Human Rights Act 1998 (HRA 1998), freedom
of speech existed when statute or common law
rules did not restrict its exercise. A.V. Dicey[6]
has in fact suggested that while French and
Belgian laws frequently made special provision for the protection (or regulation of the
press), English law was largely silent on issues

of 'freedom of speech' or 'liberty of the press'. He further argued that in England of that period, freedom of expression was no more than the right to write or say anything, which a jury, consisting of 12 shoppers, would believe was appropriate to say or write. Dicey's position is however not shared by a number of legal scholars. Barendt for instance noted that even before the HRA 1998, English courts have often invoked common law principles of freedom of speech or freedom of the press to limit the scope of other common law rules, which inhibit the exercise of these freedoms, particularly in cases of libel, breach of confidence and contempt of court.[7] It would in fact seem that judges were in the 1980s and early 1990s already being influenced by the UK participation in the European Convention despite the fact that its provisions were at that time not binding on them. A case in point was *Derbyshire City Council v Times Newspapers* [1992][8] where the Court of Appeal held that the courts were required to consider the ECHR when the common law was uncertain. In effect English common law by the 1980s and early 1990s no longer treated freedom of speech as a residual liberty but as a legal principle to which the courts must pay attention such as when they consider defences to an action for libel or breach of confidence or contempt of court.

The Human Rights Act 1998

The HRA 1998 incorporated into the UK law the rights guaranteed by the ECHR, otherwise known as the 'Convention rights.' Article 10 (1) of the European Convention on Human Rights (ECHR) states:

> Everyone has the right to freedom of expression. This right shall include freedom to hold opinions and to receive and impart information and ideas without interference by public authority and regardless of frontiers. This Article shall not prevent States from requiring the licensing of broadcasting, television or cinema enterprises.[9]

Article 10(2), of ECHR however lists conditions under which interference with the guarantees of freedom of expression under Article 10 (1) could be justified.

> The exercise of these freedoms, since it carries with it duties and responsibilities, may be subject to such formalities, conditions, restrictions or penalties as are prescribed by law and are necessary in a democratic society, in the interests of national security, territorial integrity or public safety, for the prevention of disorder or crime, for the protection of health or morals, for the protection of the reputation or rights of others, for preventing the disclosure of information received in confidence, or for maintaining the authority and impartiality of the judiciary.[10]

The incorporation of the HRA 1998 into the UK law makes it unlawful for public bodies to act incompatibly with a Convention right, though individuals and private institutions are not bound in this way.[11]Thus while freedom of speech was invariably treated as "a *defence* or an *exception or qualification* to other well-established legal rights such as the right to reputation or fair trial rights",[12] with the incorporation of the HRA 1998 into UK law, these altered considerably with the explicit provision of a right to freedom of expression in the HRA 1998. The government also added what became section 12 of the HRA to give the media and other media defendants special protection, and which appears to give some priority to freedom of expression over competing rights such as the protection of reputation.[13]

A major case to consider the implications of the convention right to freedom of expression following the HRA 1998 was *R v Shay[14]*. At issue here was the compatibility of the Official Secrets Act 1989 with freedom of expression, especially as the legislation did not recognise public interest as a defence. Following a number of European Court rulings, the House of Lords held that the key issue was whether the "restrictions imposed by the 1989 legislation were disproportionate, that is, whether they went further than necessary to safeguard national security"[15] and held that they did not.

The House noted that the legislation did not impose an absolute ban because it allowed security agents and other civil servants limited opportunities to "raise their concerns with appropriate officials or to apply for permission to disclose them to a wider audience."[16]

There have also been instances where the courts have vigorously defended press freedom after the incorporation. A good example is the A v B plc case where Lord Woolf CJ stated that any interference with press freedom has to be justified whether the particular publication was in the public interest or not.[17]

In summary, we agree with Conor Gearty that the HRA 1998, while a very important milestone in English free speech jurisprudence, does not invest an absolutist statement of rights but a mixture of civil libertarian building blocks towards democratic society's recognition of individual dignity and respect for the democratic process[18]. However, with the increasing consolidation in the media sector, which is making the media houses extremely powerful and more intrusive, the question arises of whether individuals are sufficiently being protected, especially given their unequal access to the media to put their case across, and the prohibitive costs - in both time and money – of mounting legal challenges, to protect one's privacy or reputation.

Freedom of Speech in American Jurisprudence

The love of freedom is central to the American struggle for independence. The First Amendment states:

> Congress shall make no law ... abridging the freedom of speech, or of the press, or the rights of the people peaceably to assemble, and to petition the government for a redress of grievances.[19]

The First Amendment itself is part of the United States' Bill of Rights, which among other provisions, prevents the United States Congress from making laws that infringe on the freedom of speech, or the freedom of the press or limits the right to assemble peaceably, or the right to petition the government for a redress of grievances[20]. Although the First Amendment explicitly prohibits the Congress from abridging the rights in the Bill of Rights, the courts have interpreted it as applying more broadly to both the executive and legislative branches of government[21]. Similarly in the 20th century the Supreme Court has held that the Due Process Clause of the Fourteenth Amendment "incorporates" the limitations of the First Amendment, meaning that the restrictions of the First Amendment also apply to the states, including the local governments within each of those states.[22] Zechariah Chafee Jr., a seminal modern scholar of First Amendment, has argued that the framers of the First Amendment's protection of freedom of expression intended to wipe the common law of sedition and make prosecutions for criticisms of government, without any incitement to lawbreaking, forever impossible in the United States of America.[23] In fact following *Gitlow v. New York*[24], it became generally accepted that freedom of speech and of the press are fundamental personal rights that should be protected from invasion by the states under the Due Process Clause of the Fourteenth Amendment.

Some members of the US Supreme Court have tended to take a distinctive approach to free speech issues. R.C. Post has in fact drawn attention to some incompatibilities between free speech theories and particular doctrines and decisions of the Court.[25] What is discernible from the rulings of the Court is the construction of a hierarchy of speeches in which some appear to enjoy more protection than others. As Eric Barendt puts it:

> ... the argument from democracy has been the most popular positive justification for the place of freedom of speech in US constitutional law, its influence being shown by the particularly strong protection given to political speech. In comparison, the Court has been more willing to countenance restrictions on commercial speech and advertising.[26]

Barendt notes further that rights-based arguments arising from fundamental human rights to dignity and self-fulment have not played a substantial part in shaping Supreme Court rulings on free speech, noting a tendency to treat, for example hardcore pornography, as theoretically falling outside the scope of free speech.[27]

It follows therefore that the US Supreme Court does not take an absolutist position on free speech because of vital interests that may be threatened by unrestricted speech, and also because the regulation or even the prohibition of speech may be necessary to protect the free speech right of others.[28] Interests that are often considered and balanced with free speech include public order and decency, national security, the rights to reputation and fair trial or the famous "clear and present danger" formula.[29]

In the US, one of the limits to free speech is the 'state action' doctrine, under which constitutional rights are only guaranteed against invasion by government and public authorities, including courts, but not against the decisions of private institutions and individuals. For instance in *Columbia Broadcasting System v Democratic National Committee*[30], the Supreme Court held that the private broadcasting company CBS did not violate freedom of speech by its refusal to allow the political group DNC advertising time to protest against the conduct of the Vietnam war. In *Lloyds Corporation v Tanner,*[31] the Supreme Court similarly held that the owners of a shopping mall did not violate free speech by refusing to permit demonstration on their property.

In essence the US courts do not take an absolutist position on free speech as famously advocated by Black J, a member of the Supreme court from 1937 to 1971, as such a position would be almost impossible to sustain because of interests that could be threatened by unrestricted free speech such as the need to protect the free speech rights of others or to protect reputation. One of the balancing tests of course is the famous 'clear and present' danger formula cited earlier under which free speech could be curtailed only when such speech is aimed at producing imminent lawless behaviour and likely to produce it.[32] Under this test for instance, insulting and inflammatory speeches are protected unless the state can show that such speeches present 'clear and imminent' danger of leading to lawlessness. Thus, in *RAV v St Paul*[33], the Court struck down a city ordinance, which penalised extreme hate speech on the grounds of the victim's race, colour, creed, religion or gender on the grounds that such would amount to prohibiting speech simply because of its content.

Again in *Miami Herald v. Tornillo³⁴*, the Supreme Court invalidated a statutory right of
reply to critical newspaper articles on the argument that it violated press freedom. Similarly in the famous *Pentagon Papers³⁵* case, it
was held that courts in the US are not allowed
to grant prior restraint unless that state can
show that without such a restraint, it would
suffer immediate and irreparable danger.

A major underlying principle of the US free
speech jurisprudence is a strong suspicion of
government, including its motive, for any attempt to restrict speech. It also appears that
there is a similar distrust of lower state courts,

> "...which cannot be relied upon, it seems, to
> uphold freedom of speech when it is balanced
> against, say, the common law right to reputa-
> tion or privacy or important public interests.
> That is why the Supreme Court has formulated
> a number of free speech rules and principles,
> which must be followed by state courts"³⁶

From the foregoing, it is obvious that freedom of speech is more vigorously protected
against government intrusion in the US than in
the UK, at least before the HRA 1998. US
courts have also grappled with free speech issues longer than courts in other jurisdictions.
For instance while the US courts have grappled
with free speech issues for nearly a hundred
years, European courts have for the most part

only been engaged with them for the last forty or fifty years.[37]

References

[1]   See Universal Declaration of Human Rights (UDHR), a declaration adopted by the United Nations General Assembly on 10 December 1948 at Palais de Chaillot, Paris

[2]   For a discussion of these, see Eric Barendt, *Freedom of Speech* 2nd (Oxford: OUP, 2007), Chapter 1)

[3]   Ibid p.5

[4]   *Abrams v US* 250 US 616 630-1 (1919)

[5]   Eugene Volokh (1996) 'Freedom of Speech and the Constitutional Tension Method' in http://www.law.ucla.edu/volokh/tension.htm (accessed August 24 2008)

[6]   A.V. Dicey (1959) *Introduction to the study of the Law of the Constitution* 10th edition (London, Macmillan) ch. VI

[7]   Eric Barendt, Op Cit p. 40

[8]   *Derbyshire County Council v Times Newspapers Ltd and Others]* W.L.R. 28 *[1992]*

[9]   Cited in Fenwick and Phillipson, *Media Freedom Under the Human Rights Act*, (Oxford, Oxford University Press, 2006 p 37

[10] Cited in Ibid p.37

[11] Eric Barendt, Op Cit p. 43

[12] Ibid p.41

13   In *Douglas v Hello!* [2001] QB 967 para 133-5, Sedley LJ rejected this position, arguing that the reference to 'Convention rights' in section 12 (4) of HRA 1998 included the qualifications for the exercise of that freedom as contained in Article 10 (2).

14   *R v Shay* 1 AC 247 [2003]

15   Eric Barendt, Op Cit p.45

16   Ibid p.45

17   *A v B plc* QB 195 para 11 (iv) [2003]

18   Conor Gearty (2003) *Principles of Human Rights Adjudication* (Oxford, OUP)

19   Cited in Eric Barendt, Op Cit p. 48

20   Wkipedia, http://en.wikipedia.org/wiki/First_Amendment (Accessed 12 April 2008)

21   Ibid

22   Ibid

23   Zechariah Chafee Jr (1941) *Free Speech in the United States* (Camb, Mas) p.21

24   *Gitlow v. New York* 268 US 652, 666 [1925].

25   R.C. Post [2002] "Reconciling Theory and Doctrine in First Amendment Jurisprudence" in L.C. Bollinger and G.R. Stones (eds.) *Eternally Vigilant: Free Speech in the Modern Era* (Chicago, Chicago Univ Press,)

26   Eric Barendt, Op Cit, p.48

27   Ibid p.48

28   Ibid p.49

29   Ibid P. 50

30 *Columbia Broadcasting System v Democratic National Committee* 412 US 94 [1973]

31 *Lloyds Corporation v Tanner* 407 US 551 [1972]

32 *Brundenburg v Ohio* 395 US 444 [1969]

33 *RAV v St Paul* 505 US 377 [1992]

34 *Miami Herald v. Tornillo* 418 US 241 [1974]

35 403 US 713 [1971]

36 Eric Barendt, Op Cit p.53

37 Ibid p.55

Chapter 2

THE PROTECTION OF REPUTATION AND DEFAMATION

Introduction

It has long been recognised that the law must balance free speech rights with the right to reputation. People and companies are believed to be entitled to protect their hard-earned reputation from defamatory attacks. Protection of attacks on reputation is believed to have begun as an attempt to protect the "great men of the realm" against discomforts from stories, which might make the populace to rise against them. The fear of a possible threat to civil order arising from defaming the aristocracy made slander initially a criminal offence, which was ferociously enforced. William Prynne for instance had his ears cut off for criticising the immorality of courtiers, and when he repeated his accusation in a polemic entitled "Women Actresses – Notorious Whores," they cut off the stumps of his ears and branded his forehead with the letters, 'SL' for " seditious libeller".[1]

Tom Crone traces the origins of the laws relating to defamation to King Alfred the Great, who in the ninth century, was said to have decreed that slanderers should have their tongues cut out.[2] Shakespeare in his play *Othelo* summarised what appeared to be the social basis for the noble's obsession with protecting their reputation:

> Who steals my purse steals trash;
> 'tis something, nothing;...
> But he that filches from me my good name
> Robs me of that which not enriches him,
> And makes me poor indeed.[3]

In 1966 Justice Potter Stewart of the American Supreme Court articulated the legal rationale for defamation proceedings thus:

> The right of a man to the protection of his own reputation from unjustified invasion and wrongful hurt reflects no more than our basic concept of the essential dignity and worth of every human being – a concept at the root of any decent system of liberty.[4]

In England, the traditional method for redressing damage to reputation was duelling. However when the Star Chamber banned duelling, it permitted civil action for libel. This led to the courts being inundated with libel actions brought by insulted nobles. By the end of the 18th century there was the Fox's Libel Act, which established the rights of juries, rather than judges, to decide whether words were defamatory and put the burden of proof that the words were false, had been published or spoken maliciously and had caused real damage, on the claimant. In the 19th and 20th century, English common law appeared fashioned to serve the Victorian club. During this period, there also emerged the idea that large sums of money must be awarded to compensate gentlemen for damage to their reputation or for words, which "tend to lower them in the estimation of right-thinking members of society". Libel damages became therefore based on the evaluation of the monetary worth of a person's reputation and dignity rather than being used to punish a publisher for an error.[5] It became as Robertson and Nicol noted, a

> "a method for deciding whether the claimant really was a gentleman (one leading case involved allegations of cheating at cards, another of shooting foxes ... a gentleman hunts it down with dogs). Public men had a social obligation to clear their name from calumny... the judges helped these upper class claimants by "creating presumptions" that any slur on their character must be false, published maliciously and would do their reputations serious damage in "right-minded society".[6]

The reversal of the burden of proof invariably meant that potential libellers, essentially the emerging press, published defamatory allegations at their own peril. The law was therefore skewed, with reputation triumphing over free speech. Assertions of fact had to be proved, without any public interest defence, unless made on an occasion of privilege such as a debate in parliament or by sworn evidence in court. Libel suits are pretty expensive and wholly unpredictable and publishers generally complain that libels (or fear of libel) have a 'chilling effects' on free speech.

Defamation: Meaning

In defamation, the law recognises two torts – libel and slander. The main difference between the two lies in the medium in which the alleged defamatory statement is published. If the alleged defamatory material is made in writing or some other permanent form such as on a tape recorder, then it is libel. If however the damaging material was published in a transient form, for example simply by word of mouth, the injured party could sue for slander. In libel, the law presumes that the defamed has suffered damage and the claimant does not need to prove any financial loss. In slander however, the claimant will have to satisfy the court that he or she has suffered financial damage arising from the defamatory statement.[7]

The law makes a distinction between a defamatory allegation for which a claimant may sue in libel and remarks or insults, which however offensive or abusive are not actionable. A claimant could in principle only bring proceedings for those allegations, which infringe on his right to reputation. Usually the crucial question is: are the particular words in the context in which they are used defamatory? Words, and the way they are used, are therefore the essence of the tort of defamation and the claimant must in his statement of claim set out the words (i.e. the 'sting') of which he complains of or his claim will fail.

But what is defamation? There is no general agreement on what it means as the case law shows. For instance in *Youssoupoff v MGM Pictures Ltd*[8] Natasha, a Russian princess claimed that she had been libelled in the film, *Rasputin the Mad Monk,* produced by the defendants because a character identifiable in the film as the Princess had been seduced or raped by Rasputin. Slesser LJ held that in considering the question of whether she had been defamed or not, it would be defamatory "if it brings the plaintiff into hatred, ridicule or contempt by reason of some moral discredit on her part but also if it tends to make the plaintiff to be shunned and avoided". She was awarded £25,000 in damages. In *Sim v Stretch*[9] Lord Atkins admitted that there was no satisfactory definition of defamation and held that the traditional view that defamation was something that exposes the victim to 'hatred, ridicule, or contempt', was too narrow. He preferred the view that defamation is something that "tends to lower the claimant in the estimation of right-thinking members of society".

One general point that is established is that allegations are assessed by reference to the standards of 'right-thinking' members of the society. It will therefore not be considered libellous to suggest that one has reported a crime to the police even if such an allegation leads to one being shunned by one's colleagues. A good illustration of this is in *Byrne v Deane*[10] where the majority of the Court of Appeal ruled that a member of a golf club could not sue in libel in respect of the allegation that he had reported the club to the police for keeping illegal gambling machine in the premises.

It is important to mention that in English jurisprudence whether a statement is capable of bearing a defamatory meaning is a question of law, to be decided by the judge, while whether it actually bore the alleged meaning is a question for the jury to decide. Making a false statement about someone is not necessarily libellous. It however becomes libellous when it damages the person's reputation. The classical defences for libel actions include justification (truth), fair comment and publications done on occasions of either absolute or qualified privilege.[11]

Libel or slander could be distinguished from malicious falsehood. We have for instance noted that for a course of action to arise in libel a claimant must show that he or she is a victim of false words, which have damaging effects on his or her reputation. For instance if the alleged words caused damage but in fact had no effect on the person's reputation such as a false allegation that a man has closed down his business, the victim of such an allegation cannot make a successful claim in libel unless the person can prove that the allegation has lowered his reputation in the estimation of "right-thinking" members of the society or has caused him to be shunned and avoided. The claimant may however still obtain a legal remedy in an action for *malicious falsehood*. But to succeed here the claimant must establish three key points – that the words were false, that they were published maliciously (i.e. through spite, dishonesty, avarice or some other improper motive) and that they caused the plaintiff financial loss or capable of causing financial loss.[12] It is generally believed that in practice it is more difficult to succeed in proceedings for malicious falsehood than it is to succeed in libel or slander.

In libel, the law presumes that the alleged defamatory words are false and the onus is on the defendant to prove otherwise or that the words did not bear the alleged defamatory meanings or is published on an occasion of privilege. In actions for malicious falsehood however the burden of proof is completely reversed. The claimant has to establish both the falsity of the words and the malice of the defendant. Additionally the claimant must also show that he has lost or likely to lose financially because of the defendant's statements. Again while actions for libel or slander are usually decided by a court consisting of a judge and jury, proceedings for malicious falsehood are heard by a judge sitting alone. It should be important to bear in mind that actions for defamation and malicious falsehood are not always mutually exclusive and could overlap because there are certain occasions when a false statement is both libellous and malicious falsehood.

References

1   Geoffrey Robertson and Andrew Nicol (2002): *Media Law* (London Penguin 4th edition) p.73

2   Tom Crone (1995) *Law and the Media* (Oxford, Focal Press, Third edition) p.1

3   Cited in Ibid p.1

4   Cited in Ibid p.1

5   Geoffrey Robertson and Andrew Nicol Op Cit p.74

6   Ibid 74

7   The exceptions are slanderous statements which impute the commission of a crime punishable by imprisonment, imputing that a person has a contagious or infectious disease, suggesting adultery or unchastity in a woman and disparaging a person in his or her business, calling or profession (See Tom Crone, Op Cit p.4)

8   *Youssoupoff v MGM Pictures Ltd* 50 T.L.R. 581[1934]

9   *Sim v Stretch* 52 T.L.R 669[1936]

10 *Byrne v Deane 1 K.B. 818[1937]*

11 Geoffrey Robertson and Andrew Nicol Op Cit 108-151. See also David Price (2001) *Defamation: Law, Procedure and Practice* (London, Sweet & Maxwell, second edition) pp49-166

12 Tom Crone, Op Cit pp4-5

Chapter 3

PUBLIC INTEREST

Public Interest: meaning

In general, the notion of 'public interest is used synonymously with "common well-being", the 'common good', and the 'general welfare'. However given the increasing diversity of most societies, not just in class terms but also in racial, sociological and cultural terms, there is a general lack of consensus on what is in the 'public interest' even though it is central to policy debates, politics, democracy and the nature of government itself. A crucial question here is how many members of the public have to benefit from an action or policy before such is declared to be in the public interest? There is also the question of whether what is in the interest of the majority in a society, or a section of it, could be called 'public interest', if it is accepted that the whole notion of human rights is based on protecting the individual from the tyranny of the majority. In fact arguments that try to subordinate individual rights to the collective whim under the guise of public interest echoes Schauser's caustic remarks:

> Increases in knowledge that admittedly increase
> the pleasure of the knower are necessarily valu-
> able only under a theory that treats pleasurable
> punchings of others as valuable...[1]

The media often uses the notion of 'public interest' to justify the publication of sometimes extremely contentious material, even when such publications are only cleverly aimed at achieving a 'scoop', and promoting the commercial interests of the media house in question. Despite these reservations, public interest defence has long been regarded by the common law as a basic right, long before the emergence of human rights conventions. As far back as 1863 for instance, Crompton J. observed in *Campbell v. Spottiswoode*[2] that "it is the right of all the Queen's subjects to discuss public matters". Similarly, the defence of fair comment in libel can only succeed if the comment is on a matter of public interest. Lord Denning M.R in *London Artists Ltd. v. Littler* defined the term thus:

> "Whenever a matter is such as to affect people
> at large, so that they may be legitimately inter-
> ested in, or concerned at what is going on; or
> what may happen to them or others; then it is a
> matter of public interest on which everyone is
> entitled to make fair comment"[3].

For Roberts and Nicol:

> The courts have held that the public is legitimately interested, not merely in the conduct of public officials and institutions, but of private companies whose activities affect individual members of the public. The conduct of a professional person towards a client or an employer towards a worker are also matters that may attract legitimate public interest. Anyone who throws a hat into a public arena must be prepared to have it mercilessly, though not maliciously, trampled upon[4].

Tom Crone has rightly noted the importance of context in any definition of 'public interest', arguing that the meaning will be contextually determined. As he puts it:

> In the privacy field, it is likely to be between the public interest in protecting confidentiality, whether personal or commercial, and the public interest in publishing information, i.e. utilising the right of free expression and free speech.[5]

A good case of public interest defence is in *Lion Laboratories v Evans*[6], where two former employees of Lion Laboratories leaked information to the press based upon confidential company documents. The leaked documents showed that the company, which made breath-testing equipment, was aware that there were doubts about the accuracy and reliability of its instruments. The court held that injunctions granted to the company to prevent publication of the information should be lifted because it was in 'public interest' to publish such confidential information and noted that it was 'well accepted' that there was a public interest defence to actions of breach of confidence and breach of copyright. In the same case, Lord Justice Stephenson noted four important considerations in the identification of what should constitute the 'public interest'

1) There is a wide difference between what is interesting to the public and what is in the public interest to make known.

2) The media have a private interest of their own in publishing what appeals to the public and may increase the circulation or the numbers of their viewers or listeners and as a result they are 'particularly vulnerable to the error of confusing the public interest with their own interest'.

3) The public interest may be best served by an informer giving not to the press but to the police or other responsible body.

4) It is in the public interest to disclose grave misconduct or wrongdoing or to put it another way there is no confidence 'as to the disclosure of iniquity.[7]

It is germane to note that in libel, the defence of fair comment on matters of public interest must relate to *comment*, and not to statements of fact, which must be justified' (i.e. proved to be true). One of the major difficulties here is when facts and opinions are jumbled together in the same article or programme because words, which in one context are opinions (and therefore defensible as "fair comment") could in another context appear as factual statements (which, would as a defence, require proof of correctness or justification). The test on whether such could be categorised as comments or as statement of facts would be with reference to the ordinary readers: would they on reading or hearing such regard them as comments or as a statement of facts?

A good illustration of how it could sometimes be difficult to separate factual comments from opinions is in *Telnikoff v Matusevitch*[8]. Here the claimant had written an article in the *Daily Telegraph* criticising the BBC for recruiting mainly members of the USSR's national minorities for its Russia service. The defendant wrote a "letter to the editor", in response, describing the claimant's views as racist and anti-Semitic. The claimant sued. At issue was whether the words used in the 'letter to the editor' could be construed as factual statements or as opinions. The House of Lords reversed a ruling by the Court of Appeal and ruled that the jury should be permitted to look at the 'letter to the editor' independent of the original article (which made the words complained of to appear like factual statements). Though this decision has been justifiably criticised, in part because letters to the editor are generally written and read as comments, it does buttress the difficulties that could sometimes arise in separating comments from factual statements.

Essential elements of Public Interest

We will look at three key elements that often come into play in the discussions of public interest in the law of defamation – public officials, public figures and malice. The first two come into play for their roles in generating activities that are deemed to be in public interest[9], while malice comes into play in proceedings in which public interest is used by the media as a defence. Generally a proof that a publication is actuated by malice will defeat the defence, even if it is accepted that the publication is in public interest.

Public figures

For a person to be considered a public figure, he or she is expected to be engaged in a fairly high threshold of public activity. Typically, they must either be a public figure, or a public official or any other person pervasively involved in public affairs, or a 'limited purpose public figure', meaning those who have immersed themselves to the forefront of particular public controversies in a bid to influence the resolution of the issues involved. A "particularized determination" is usually required to decide whether a person is a limited purpose public figure, which can be variously interpreted.[10] One can also be an 'involuntary limited-purpose public figure' – for example, an air traffic controller on duty at the time of a fatal crash would be an involuntary, limited-purpose public figure, because the media will likely focus on him for an eye witness account of that public occurrence.[11] Media focus on such people often unwittingly lead to their being profiled, and given the competition among the media houses for scoops, even what ought to be treated as private information about such figures, would be brought to the public domain, especially those that are sensational or would help in selling more copies or attracting more viewers.

It is generally accepted that while a public figure is entitled to a private life and should have his privacy respected in appropriate circumstances, he must also accept that because he is in the 'eyes of the public', the public may have a legitimate and understandable interest in being told some otherwise private information about him. In *AvB*[12], for instance, the Court of Appeal held that a public figure should recognise that because of his public position, he must expect and accept that his actions will be more closely scrutinised by the media, especially if they are held as role models. A similar approach was

33

els. A similar approach was taken in *Theakston v MGN[13]*, where the TV presenter Jamie Theakson, sought to restrain both photographs and a story giving details of his encounter with prostitutes in a brothel. The judge granted an injunction restraining the use of the photograph but refused to injunct the story partly on the grounds of its public interest.

One of the common arguments by the media is that if they do not publish information which the public are interested in, there will be fewer newspapers published, which will not be in the public interest. But a legitimate question may be raised, for instance, about whether the public really deserves to know about a public figure's private liaisons with a prostitute in so far as this was not done with public resources, and such private actions, however morally reprehensible, do not detract from the public figure's (or even public official's) ability to do his public functions. The media's use of public interest defence is even more controversial when they intrude into the private lives of certain categories of public officials. One of such categories could be the "involuntary public figure", that is, a person who became a 'public figure' as the result of unwanted publicity. A good example here is 'Joe the Plumber'[14], who, in the US presidential campaigns between Barrack Obama and John McCain in 2008 quickly became a symbol of the American self-made man's resistance to progressive taxation. The story began on 12 October 2008, outside Toledo, Ohio, USA. As Senator Barrack Obama campaigned for the Presidency in a neighbourhood of modest homes, a man named Samuel J. (Joe) Wurzelbacher (alias Joe the Plumber) approached him. He said that he was getting ready to buy a company that earned about a quarter of a million dollars a year, and asked if his taxes would rise under Obama's economic plan. The Senator acknowledged that they might. During the last presidential debate between John McCain and Barrack Obama on October 16, 2008, McCain brought up Joe's supposed worries about Obama's proposed tax rates for wealthy Americans and accused Obama of waging "class warfare." His name was invoked 12 times during the debate and Joe the Plumber suddenly became a national figure, with reporters camping in his home to interview him.

However as Joe the Plumber suddenly became transformed into an involuntary public figure overnight, with networks offering him interviews, it was also quickly discovered that Wurzelbacher was not everything he seemed: he did not hold a licence to perform plumbing or contracting work; a lien had been filed against him for non-payment of taxes; and he admitted that he lied when he claimed to

Obama that he was expecting to enter the high tax bracket ($250,000 and above). The crucial question here is whether the issues that were being dug up against Joe the Plumber were really of public interest, given that he was a private citizen, had merely asked a presidential candidate a question about his proposed tax plan, and had become a public figure, most probably against his wish[15]. Here an aspect of the public interest defence often exploited by the opposition press was the 'need to put the record straight', for, among other things, 'Joe the Plumber' had lied he was about to enter the high-income bracket when he was not, and was also a registered Republican who could have been planted by the GOP to ask Senator Obama the question, and later accused him of "a socialist agenda", and of wanting to "spread the wealth around".

The case of Joe the Plumber therefore raises the question of whether the private information of involuntary public officials (such as about their taxes or finances), which may be of interest to the media and the public, can really be said to be in the public interest.

There are instances in which the courts have taken the position that certain people in the 'eyes of the public' are not public figures, and that information about them, which could be interesting to the public, are not really of public interest. A case in point is *McKennitt v*

Ash.[16] In this case a former friend of McKennitt, a reputed folk singer, wanted to publish a revealing book about the singer's life. McKennitt sought an injunction and damages for breach of confidence. The trial judge argued that there was little public interest in the revelations in the book, and no public interest that could outweigh the singer's privacy rights as guaranteed by Art 8 of the European Convention on Human Rights. Ms Ash however argued that McKennitt was a public figure and "for that reason alone", there was a legitimate public interest in her affairs. In rejecting Ms Ash's argument, the Court of Appeal expressed surprise that McKennit should be considered a public figure. The court followed the European jurisprudence from the Court of Human Rights, which held that that while the press has an:

> ... important role... in dealing with matters of public interest... a distinction was then to be drawn between the watchdog role in the democratic process and the reporting of private information about people who, although of interest to the public, were not public figures.[17]

It follows from the above that what could be said to be in the public interest is often subjectively determined. Even certain activities of private individuals could be of public interest. A less subjective approach in determining the public interest would perhaps be to develop a taxonomy of what constitutes 'public interest', along the lines of the one adopted in the Code of Practice of the Press Complaints Commission, to which the courts are directed under 12 HRA[18] to have regards to in cases involving free speech interests. The Code of Practice gives a non-exhaustive list of what 'public interest' entails:

1. The public interest includes, but is not confined to:
    i) Detecting or exposing crime or serious impropriety.
    ii) Protecting public health and safety.
    iii) Preventing the public from being misled by an action or statement of an individual or organisation.
2. There is a public interest in freedom of expression itself.
3. Whenever the public interest is invoked, the PCC will require editors to demonstrate fully how the public interest was served.
4. The PCC will consider the extent to which material is already in the public domain, or will become so.
5. In cases involving children under 16, editors must demonstrate an exceptional public interest to over-ride the normally paramount interest of the child[19].

Public Officials

Article 2A of the United Nations Anti-Corruption Convention defines a "Public official" as "any person holding a legislative, executive, administrative or judicial office, whether appointed or elected; any other person who performs a public function or provides a public service; any other person defined as a public official in the domestic law."[20] For the African Union, a public official means "any official or employee of the State or its agencies including those who have been selected, appointed or elected to perform activities or functions in the name of the state or in the service of the State at any level of its hierarchy"[21]

There is really no difference between these two definitions. What is clear is that 'public officials' are narrower in the scope of their activities than public figures in that their official functions are tied to the state, or carried out on behalf of the state or its agency. For this reason it is easy to surmise that their official activities are of public interest as they work – whether paid or voluntary- on behalf of the state. But could one also argue that their private activities are not really of public interest? Does the public have the right to know of a public official, especially a high-ranking one, who engages in scandalous activities in his private life (e.g. sex tours or involvement in prostitution ring)?

What should be the basis of the public's right to know of such private activities, no matter how scandalous, if they do not affect the public official's capacity to discharge his or her duty? How should we determine when a public official's private activities affect his ability to perform his public functions, and thus making those private activities matters of public interest?

Malice

In defamation cases, many of the important defences available to the media could be defeated if the claimant successfully proves that the publication was actuated by malice. Though ordinarily the term malice means 'spite', or 'ill-will', in libel it generally refers to "dishonest or reckless writing or reporting – the publication of facts that are known or suspected to be false, or opinions that are not genuinely held."[22] The existence of these qualities however is not enough proof of malice and the burden of proof is on the claimant. As Robertson and Nicol noted:

> ... the mere existence of personal antagonism between writer and claimant will not defeat a legitimate defence if the published criticism, however intemperate, is an honest opinion.[23]

Malice has therefore a broader meaning in law than it has in every day language. In

Horrocks v Lowe[24], for instance the House of Lords underlined the importance of the legal meaning of malice in a case, which arose during a council meeting. In that meeting, Lowe, a Labour councillor, had launched an intemperate attack on Horrocks, a Tory councillor, whose company had land dealings with the Tory-controlled local authority. Speeches during such occasions are normally protected by qualified privilege (but such a defence will crumble if the claimant successfully proves that the defendant was motivated by malice). The trial judge however found that though Lowe's political antagonism with Horrocks had inflamed his mind into a state of "gross and unreasoning prejudice", he genuinely believed that every allegation he levelled against Horrocks was true. Based on that, the House of Lords held that Lowe was not "malicious" in law. In ordinary sense of the word, it would be easy to prove that Lowe was malicious.

A passage from Lord Diplock's in *Horrocks v Lowe* is generally believed to be the classical exposition of the legal meaning of malice.

> "What is required on the part of the defamer to entitle him to the protection of the privilege is positive belief in the truth of what he published...if he publishes untrue defamatory matter recklessly, without considering or caring whether it be true or not, he is in this, as in other branches of the law, treated as if he knew

it to be false. But indifference to the truth of what he publishes is not to be equated with carelessness, impulsiveness or irrationality in arriving at positive belief that it was true. The freedom of speech protected by the law of qualified privilege may be availed of by all sorts and conditions of men. In affording to them immunity from suit if they acted in good faith in compliance with a legal or moral duty or in protection of a legitimate interest, the law must take them as it finds them...In greater or less degree according to their temperaments, their training, their intelligence, they are swayed by prejudice, rely on intuition instead of reasoning, leap to conclusion on inadequate evidence and fail to recognise the cogency of material which might cast doubt on the validity of the conclusions they reach. But despite the imperfection of the mental process by which the belief is arrived at, it may still be honest', that is a positive belief that the conclusions they have reached are true. The law demands no more"[25]

Robertson and Nicol have noted that malice has a different nuance when it is used in the defence of fair comment from when it is used in defence of qualified privilege[26]. In fair comment defence, the claimant must prove dishonesty or at least a reckless disregard for the truth on the part of the defendant in order to defeat the claim. Here the defendant's *actual malice* (his spite or hatred of the claimant) will not be enough to negate the defence provided he honestly believed in the opinions he expressed. But in qualified privilege, the defence will be lost if it is proved that the defendant misused the occasion of publication for an ulterior and vicious purpose, even though he believed at the time of publication in the truth of the publication, which have turned out to be false.

While recklessness to the truth or falsity of accusations may amount to malice, carelessness, impulsiveness or irrationality do not. Similarly lack of care for the consequences of exuberant reporting, mere inaccuracy or a failure to make inquiries or accidental or negligent misquotations are not sufficient to prove malice[27]. To successfully prove malice in such situations, the claimant must show that not only that the defendant has turned a blind eye to the truth but also that he did so in a bid to advance an ulterior motive. A good case in point here is *Royal Aquarium v Parkinson*[28]. In this case Parkinson, a Victorian clean-up campaigner, who had a strong moral objection to "public dancing", alleged that a ballet at the Royal Aquarium had involved a Japanese female catching a butterfly "in the most indecent place you could possibly imagine". However when he was presented with evidence that the performer in question was neither Japanese nor female and was actually dressed in pantaloons, Parkinson confessed that he had difficulty observing the performance and that his aim in levelling the allegation was simply to have the Aquarium's dancing licence revoked. His malice destroyed the privilege to which he would have otherwise been entitled.

Malice remains difficult to prove, despite efforts to 'objectify' it by developing a checklist of responsible journalism – as we shall see later. The burden of proof of malice is on the claimant, which while furthering the cause of press freedom can sometimes make it very difficult for an individual to successfully seek legal remedy for damaged reputation.

References

1   F Schauser (1999), "Reflections on the Value of Truth" 41 *Case Western Reserve Law Review* 699, p. 711

2   *Campbell v. Spottiswoode* (1863) 3 B. & S. 769, 779,

3   *London Artists Ltd. v. Littler* 2 Q.B. 375, 391 [1969]

4   Geoffrey Robertson and Andrew Nicol Op Cit pp124-125

5   Tom Crone, Op Cit p.17

6   *Lion Laboratories v Evans* 2 All E.R 417 [1984]

7   Ibid at p 423

8   *Telnikoff v Matusevitch*, 2 A.C. 343 [1992]

9   Private individuals also generate matters of public interest but for obvious reasons the media are

more easily attracted by the activities of 'public figures' and 'public officials'.

[10] Wikipedia (http://en.wikipedia.org/wiki/Public_fi gure, accessed October 5, 2008)

[11] Electronic Frontier Foundation – Bloggers' FAQ: Online Defamation Law (http://w2.eff.org/blog gers/lg/faq-defamation.php#7, accessed October 5, 2008)

[12] *A v B plc* 3 WLR 542[2002] at para 11 (xii)

[13] *Theakston v MGN* EMLR 22 [2002]

[14] See for instance 'Overtaxed: The story of Joe the plumber' in The *New Yorker, October 20, 2008* (http://www.msnbc.msn.com/id/27276 786/ accessed, October 20 2008)

[15] Joe the Plumber later appeared on the campaign trail with the Republican presidential candidate John McCain and permitted the party to use his name in political ads criticising Senator Barrack Obama's tax plans. He was also quoted as indicating an interest in running for Congress. His increasing involvement in politics could in these circumstances mean that he is no longer an 'involuntary public figure' and justify the press interest in his private affairs as being in the 'public interest'.

[16] *McKennitt v Ash* EWHC 3003 [2005]

[17] [2006] ECWA 171 at para. 58

[18] per ss (1), s 12 applies whenever the court is considering granting any relief which would affect the European Convention Right to freedom of expression.

[19] Press Complaints Commission: Code of Practice (http://www.pcc.org.uk/cop/practice.html accessed, October 27, 2008)

[20] U4-Anti Corruption Resource Centre (http://www.u4.no/themes/conventions/convdefpublic official.cfm, Accessed October 20, 2008)

[21] Ibid

[22] Geoffrey Robertson and Andrew Nicol Op Cit p.110

[23] Ibid p.110

[24] *Horrocks v Lowe,* AC 135[1975] [at 149]

[25] Ibid [at 149]

[26] Geoffrey Robertson and Andrew Nicol Op Cit p.111

[27] Ibid p.111

[28] *Royal Aquarium and Summer and Winter Garden Society Ltd v Parkinson* 1 QB 431, C.A. [1892]

Chapter 4

FREE SPEECH, PROTECTION OF REPUTATION, AND PUBLIC INTEREST DEFENCE IN AMERICAN LAW OF DEFAMATION: CASE LAW

Introduction

In the United States and to a less extent many common law jurisdictions, there is a clear trend in the past few decades to give increasing protection to freedom of speech at the expense of rights or interests in reputation or privacy. This marked a departure from the era when the United States Supreme Court did not consider defamation to be 'speech' protected by the First Amendment, but was rather to be equated with an assault.[1] In fact until recently reputation was one of the fundamental liberties protected by the Due Process Clause of the Fourteenth Amendment to the United States' Constitution.[2]

In trying to balance free speech rights with the need to protect reputation, the US courts do not weigh the competing interests in a case-by-case ad hoc way, or within the framework of a general rule such as the 'clear and present danger' test.[3] The US Supreme Court rather formulated a number of precise rules to cover actions for libel under which the First Amendment protects speech, which might otherwise attract defamation proceedings. M.B. Nimmer has argued that this 'definitional' balancing approach ensures greater predictability of decisions and enables the courts to give greater weight to free speech rights than would have been possible under an ad hoc approach.[4]

Increasingly the US Courts have accepted that the press and other media should be given the right to publish defamatory allegations about the conduct of politicians and other leading figures provided that such stories are of 'public interest' and that the publisher has not acted irresponsibly. We will examine some cases in which 'public interest' played a key role either in the media's defence of its attack on reputation or in a judgment resulting from court proceedings from such an attack to see how the notion is defined and balanced with the need to protect reputation and the individual from press tyranny.

New York Times Co. v. Sullivan[5]

A landmark case in this regard is *New York Times Co. v. Sullivan*. The case's antecedent was *Brown v. Board of Education of Topeka*[6], in which the United States Supreme Court overturned earlier rulings going back to *Plessy v Ferguson*[7] in 1896. In the latter case the

Court had upheld the constitutionality of racial segregation even in public accommodations (especially railroads), under a so-called doctrine of "separate but equal". The decision, which was handed down by a vote of 7 to 1, remained the standard doctrine in U.S. law until its final repudiation by the Supreme Court's decision in *Brown v. Board of Education,* which by (9-0) decision stated that "separate educational facilities are inherently unequal" and that state laws that established separate public schools for black and white students denied black children equal educational opportunities.

It is important to understand the global political environment that perhaps influenced the *Brown v Board of Education* decision. The end of the Second World War had unleashed a powerful wave of anti-colonial struggles by many developing countries, especially in Africa. The anti-colonial movements, often with open support from Communist countries such as China or Russia, challenged the ideology of racial hierarchy, which provided one of the justifications for colonialism in the first place. There were many movements, especially Socialist and Communist parties in North America and Europe, supporting the anti-colonial movements. Domestically the civil rights movement in the US was at its apogee. Therefore a conjunction of both the civil rights struggles and the global political environment, accentuated by the fallouts of the Cold War, provided the context for the repudiation of the "separate but equal" doctrine.

Obviously not all would accept a major ideological shift of this magnitude in the US and there were allegations that many Southern states resisted the decision in *Brown v Board of Education.* Libel actions, and their threats, were allegedly used to "chill" the free reporting of the civil rights campaigns, and the resistance to the *Brown v Board of Education* decision in the Southern states. These were therefore the background to the *Sullivan* case.

On March 29, 1960, the *New York Times* carried a full-page advertisement entitled "Heed Their Rising Voices", which solicited funds to defend the civil rights leader, Martin Luther King Jr., against an Alabama tax-evasion charge. The advertisement described actions against civil rights protesters, quite a number of them inaccurately, which involved the police force of Montgomery, Alabama. Though Commissioner L. B. Sullivan, whose duties included supervision of the police department, wasn't named in the advertisement, he argued that his position as a commissioner there meant that the inaccurate criticism of the actions of the police were defamation against him.

Alabama law denied a public officer recovery of punitive damages in a libel action brought on account of a publication concerning their official conduct unless they first make a written demand for a public retraction and the defendant fails or refuses to comply. Commissioner Sullivan sent such a request but the *New York Times* refused to publish a retraction and demanded to know why Commissioner Sullivan felt the advertisement defamed him. Sullivan did not respond but instead filed a libel suit a few days later. He also sued four black ministers mentioned in the advertisement. An Alabama court ruled in his favour, and awarded him $500,000 in damages.

The US Supreme Court found the rule of law applied by the Alabama courts to be constitutionally deficient for failure to provide the safeguards for freedom of speech and of the press that are required by the First and Fourteenth Amendments. The judgement quoted approvingly Mr. Justice Brandeis, in his concurring opinion in *Whitney v. California*[8] on the need for special protection of public interest speeches:

"Those who won our independence believed . . . that public discussion is a political duty, and that this should be a fundamental principle of the American government. They recognised the risks to which all human institutions are subject. But they knew that order cannot be secured merely through fear of punishment for its infraction; that it is hazardous to discourage thought, hope and imagination; that fear breeds repression; that repression breeds hate; that hate menaces stable government; that the path of safety lies in the opportunity to discuss freely supposed grievances and proposed remedies, and that the fitting remedy for evil counsels is good ones. Believing in the power of reason as applied through public discussion, they eschewed silence coerced by law -- the argument of force in its worst form. Recognizing the occasional tyrannies of governing majorities, they amended the Constitution so that free speech and assembly should be guaranteed." [9]

The ruling in the case established the *actual malice* standard before press reports could be considered defamatory of a public official. It prohibited public officials from recovering damages for defamatory falsehood relating to their official conduct absent *actual malice*. One of the immediate consequences of the ruling was that it allowed free reporting of the civil rights campaigns in the southern United States.

The *actual malice* standard requires that the claimant in a defamation or libel case prove that the publisher of the statement in question knew that the statement was false or acted in reckless disregard of its truth or falsity. The term, *actual malice*, on face value, appears puzzling, since the standard refers to knowledge or reckless lack of investigation, not to malicious intent. This term was not invented especially for the *Sullivan* case, but was a term from existing libel law. In many jurisdictions, including Alabama (where the case arose), proof of "actual malice" was required in order for punitive damages to be awarded, or for other increased penalties. However since it is extremely difficult to provide proof of an alleged libeller's malicious intentions, proof that the writer knowingly published a falsehood was generally accepted as proof of malice, under the assumption that only a malicious person would knowingly publish a falsehood.

It is important to note from the quote from Mr. Justice Brandeis (above) the special role of 'public discussion' (i.e. discussions that are supposedly in the 'public interest'), and the dicta that public officials are fair games for media houses, if attacks on them could be justified on the grounds of public interest or if such attacks could further such an interest. To avoid giving the media an unfettered licence to attack public officials in the name of public interest, the ruling established the *actual malice* standard which has to be met before press reports about public officials (later applied to public figures) could be considered to be defamatory. In other words, while enhancing the scope of free speech it also sought to ensure a certain, if feeble, attempt to ensure that the press is not given a blank cheque. But the decision, (and the Court's implied notion 'public interest'), in the political context in which it was made, was a courageous one as it allowed the press a freer hand to report on the civil rights movements and the resistance to the *Brown v Board of Education* in some southern states like Alabama.

One significant thing about the *New York Times v Sullivan* case was that because of the extremely high burden of proof *actual malice* required of the claimant, and the difficulty in proving essentially what is inside a person's head, such cases — when they involve public figures or public officials — rarely prevail. While this may be good for free speech, it could also pose difficulties of potential press overreach, of the press substituting its interest for the public interest, and of the individual not being sufficiently protected from press assault. In fact Lee C. Bollinger[10] found that in *Mason v New Yorker Magazine* (111 S Ct 2419 [1991]), that the "press did not look very good" and the "reputation of journalism was blemished". In that case, the Court was confronted with action brought by Mason who claimed that the defendants had published an article in which he was quoted as saying things he never said. Following *New York Times v Sullivan* and its sequel, Mason who conceded to being a public figure, bore the burden of establishing that the fabricated quotes or defamatory statements were published with 'actual malice', that is with knowledge or reckless disregard of their falsity. Despite this big hurdle, the press lost the case, showing the extent to which the press could go after its own interest, with little regard for people's reputation.

Curtis Publishing Co. v. Butts[11]

The case arose from an article published in the *Saturday Evening Post,* which accused Wally Butts of attempting to fix a football game played in 1962 between the University of Georgia and the University of Alabama. Butts, who was a well-known figure within the coaching ranks and was at the time of the publication of the article an athletic director, and former coach of the University of Georgia's football team, sued Curtis Publishing Company for libel. He sought $5 million in compensatory damages and another $5 million in punitive damages.

The primary source of the article was George Burnett, an Atlanta insurance salesman. Burnett had accidentally overheard a telephone conversation, a week before the football game, between Butts and the coach of Alabama's football team, Paul Bryant. Burnett noted down the conversation in which he claimed that Butts revealed Georgia's game plans, including naming specific players and plays. Butts sued for libel and the trial was concluded before the Court ruled in the *New York Times v. Sullivan.*

The focus of the trial was on whether the article was true, and whether the reporting was accurately done. Though Burnett claimed he overheard a conversation between Butts and Bryant; what he heard was a matter of debate. Butts claimed the conversation was confined to general football talk and would have yielded little useful information to any opposing coach.

The jury ruled that in the preparation of the article, the magazine "departed greatly from the standards of good investigation and reporting" and returned a verdict of $60,000 in general damages and $3million in punitive damages against Curtis. The trial court reduced the award to $460,000. Shortly after the US Supreme Court announced the landmark *Sullivan* decision and Curtis motioned for a new trial. The trial court rejected the motion on two grounds. First, it held that *New York Times* was not applicable because Butts was not a public official; and second, there was plenty of evidence for the jury to have concluded that there was a reckless disregard for the truth.[12] Curtis appealed the ruling to the Court of Appeals for the Fifth Circuit, but the judgment was affirmed. A rehearing was denied and the Supreme Court granted *certiorari.*

The important issues in the ruling as it pertains to an assessment of public interest are:

1) The *New York Times* rule, which forbade a public official from recovering damages for defamatory falsehood relating to his official conduct, absent actual malice as therein defined, should not be inexorably applied to defamation actions by "public figures" like those here, where different considerations are present[13]. .

2) A "public figure" who is not a public official may recover damages for defamatory falsehood substantially endangering his reputation on a showing of highly unreasonable conduct constituting an extreme departure from the standards of investigation and reporting ordinarily adhered to by responsible publishers[14].

3) In view of the court's instructions, the jury must have decided that the magazine's investigation was grossly inadequate, and the evidence amply supported a finding of the highly unreasonable conduct referred to above[15].

One of the implicit recognitions in this case is that while public officials, as agents of the state can be allowed to bring defamatory proceedings, only in instances of the difficult-to-prove actual malice standard, (arguably because the state belongs to all and everything done in the name of the state is of interest to all stakeholders), 'public figures' on the other hand, cannot simply be penalised for being in

the 'eyes of the public', sometimes against
their will. Butts was employed by a private organisation, but a 'public figure' (a limited public figure by our definition) only by virtue of
his job. It is therefore right that the reputation
of such individuals should be protected
through demanding a higher standard of media
responsibility than that offered under the *New
York* standard. Were this not so, it becomes
easier for the press to capitalise on the names
of these officials to publish sensational stories
(as some tabloids still do today) under the
guise of public interest while the real interest is
their bottom line. So here again we find an
echo of Tom Jones emphasis on the importance of context in the delineation of what
should be said to be in the public interest.

It is very interesting that in this case the jury
decided, and the Court affirmed that the magazine's investigation of the case was grossly inadequate, and that it "departed greatly from the
standards of good investigation and reporting".
So instead of leaving juries to figure out what
is in someone's head (i.e. actual malice) as was
the case in the *New York* standard, there was a
pointer on how this could be assessed, and this
was by reference to 'standards of good
investigation'. It is in fact actually debatable
whether the 'actual malice' standard was the
one applied to the case because the ruling was
that a "public figure" who is not a "public
official" may recover damages for defamatory

may recover damages for defamatory false-hood, which substantially endangered his reputation "on a showing of highly unreasonable conduct constituting an extreme departure from the standards of investigation and reporting ordinarily adhered to by responsible publishers." It would seem that in this case, the requirement was for the 'public figure' to prove "irresponsible journalism' – unless this is taken to mean the same thing as "knowledge of a falsity of a story or reckless disregard of its truth". It would have of course helped if the Court had given a checklist of how "responsible" or 'irresponsible" journalism should be assessed.

The Butts ruling was actually based on two cases – *Curtis Publishing v Butts* and *Associated Press v Walker* ([1967] 389 U.S. 28). In the latter, the case arose from a press report about a riot which resulted when a black student, James Meredith, tried to integrate into the University of Mississippi under a court order. The report accused retired General Edwin Walker of leading a charge against the federal marshals and claimed that Walker encouraged the use of violence and even advised the rioters on how to avoid the harmful side effects of tear gas. At the time of the riot and press report, Walker was a private citizen. But he had had a long and distinguished career in the U.S. Army and had also been in command of general troops during the school confrontation in Little Rock, Arkansas in 1957. He had resigned his army post to become more politically active and had received some publicity on his views on integration. Walker, it could be argued, was an ex-public official, and a different kind of public figure. Walker sued for libel in the state courts of Texas seeking $2 million in compensatory and punitive damages. He disputed the facts in the wire story. He admitted that while he indeed was on the campus as reported by Associated Press, he had contrary to their report tried to keep the crowd from rioting, urging them to remain peaceful. He denied taking part in the charge against federal marshals.

In the *Associated Press v Walker* case, the AP reporter who filed the report was at the scene of the riot. There was no evidence suggesting that the article was not filed properly or any personal prejudice or incompetence on the part of the reporter. The jury was directed to award compensatory damages if the article was false, and to award punitive damages if the article was actuated by ill will, bad or evil motive or that or reckless disregard for truth. The jury returned a verdict of $500,000 in compensatory damages and $300,000 in punitive damages. The trial judge however found no evidence of actual malice and refused to enter the punitive award. The trial judge said that the lack of malice would have meant a verdict for the Associated Press, if *New York Times* were applicable. He however argued that *New York Times v Sullivan* was inapplicable and that truth should be an adequate defence.

Both sides appealed, and the Texas Court of Civil Appeals affirmed the compensatory damages and the dismissal of punitive damages. The Supreme Court of Texas denied writ of error and the U.S. Supreme Court granted *certiorari.*

It is interesting how the Supreme Court treated the two cases, despite accepting that both Butts and Walker were public figures. The majority argued that as public figures, they could recover damages once it was proven that the "standards of traditional" reporting were not followed. While it found that the standard was satisfied in *Butts,* it held that it was not satisfied in *Walker.* The Court further reasoned that unlike in *Walker,* there was no real urgency (or breaking news element) in the *Butts* case, which meant that the *Saturday Evening Post* had plenty of time to verify the facts in the article. The Court concluded that the reporting of the Butts story was sloppy despite the lack of time constraints or breaking news element in the story. Additionally during the trial Butts had submitted evidence that the *Saturday Evening Post* had instituted a policy of "sophisticated muckraking," to shore up flagging sales, and was aware that Burnett was on criminal probation – something that would have raised the alarm bell about his trustworthiness - but still went ahead and published the story without corroborating it. It also turned out that no other editor or staff of the paper reviewed Burnett's notes before publication, and the person who was supposedly with Burnett when he claimed to overhear the phone call was not interviewed. Furthermore, the writer assigned to the story was not a football expert and no attempt was made to have an expert review the story before it was published. It was therefore right for the Court to find that in the Butts case, the *Saturday Evening Post* was guilty of "highly unreasonable conduct constituting an extreme departure from the standards of investigation and reporting ordinarily adhered to by responsible publishers."

In a separate opinion, Justice Warren agreed with the outcome but disagreed with the reasoning. He placed more emphasis on the status of both Walker and Butts as public figures and reasoned that that should be the major thrust (rather than whether the press has been responsible or irresponsible in its investigation) behind the Court's ruling. Warren's position was:

> "To me, differentiations between 'public figures' and 'public officials' and adoption of separate standards of proof for each have no basis in law, logic, or First Amendment policy.

Increasingly in this country, the distinctions between governmental and private sectors are
blurred."[16]

Justice Warren's position would have made
every public official or public figure a fair
game for journalists, in the name of public interest. This would in turn have defeated the
whole notion of human rights, privacy and
reputation, and would have invited press tyranny against people in the 'eyes of the public'.

Interestingly, Justice Black joined by Justice
Douglas wrote yet another opinion agreeing
with the outcome in *Walker,* but dissented with
the majority in *Curtis.* Calling for a broader
press immunity, he argued that *Sullivan* failed
to adequately protect the press from libel
judgments and its potential chilling effects on
free speech – a position we feel would have led
to even more recklessness on the part of the
press. He would have reversed the *Butts* ruling
because the article was a matter of public
interest. Justice Brennan joined by Justice
White agreed with *Walker,* but dissented in
Butts. Brennan argued that the jury instructions
did not follow the standard for malice and
therefore the ruling should be reversed and
remanded for a new trial. He further reasoned
that the jury should have an opportunity to
determine if the *New York Times* standard was
met

Time Inc v Hill[17]

In 1952, three escaped convicts took the wife and five children of one James Hill hostage in their home in Pennsylvania. The family was released after about nineteen hours, unharmed. The convicts were later apprehended in a violent clash with police during which two of them were killed. The story made Hill and his family the subject of front-page news, transforming them over night into 'public figures'. In an interview with newsmen after the convicts had departed, Hill stressed that the convicts had treated the family courteously, had not molested them, and had not been at all violent. Shortly after, the family relocated to Connecticut and discouraged all efforts to keep them in the public spotlight through magazine articles or appearances on television.

In 1953, Joseph Hayes published a novel based on the Hill family's ordeal. When the novel was subsequently made into a play, (also authored by Hayes) *Life Magazine* ("Life") published an article about the play that mirrored many of its inaccuracies concerning the Hill family's experience. The article was published in February 1955 under the caption: "True Crime Inspires Tense Play", with the subtitle, "The ordeal of a family trapped by convicts gives Broadway a new thriller, 'The Desperate Hours.'" The pictures in the article included an enactment of the son being "roughed up" by one of the convicts, of the daughter biting the hand of a convict to make him drop a gun, and of Hill himself throwing his gun through the door after a "brave try" to save his family is foiled.

Hill alleged that *Life* deliberately misrepresented his story and sought damages against the magazine. The case was argued on 27 April 1966, reargued 18–19 Oct. 1966 and decided on 9 January 1967 by a vote of 5 to 4; Brennan for the Court, Black and Douglas concurring, Harlan concurring in part and dissenting in part, Fortas, joined by Warren and Clarke, in dissent.

The key question in the case was whether a publication, containing misrepresentations about the subject of its coverage was protected under the First Amendment's freedom of speech guarantees? The case built upon the Supreme Court's opinion in *New York Times Co. v. Sullivan*, in which the Court had held that claimants who were public officials could not recover damages for defamation unless they could demonstrate that the defamation had been published with ***actual*** *malice*.

The Court set aside the Appellate ruling against *Time* on the grounds that the lower court failed to instruct the jury that *Time's* liability was contingent upon a showing that it knowingly and recklessly published false statements about the Hill family. The Court explained that absent a finding of such malicious intent on the part of a publisher, press statements are protected under the First Amendment even if they are otherwise false or inaccurate. The Court remanded for retrial under the new jury instruction. In concurring to the majority opinion Justice Douglas said:

> The episode around which this book was written had been news of the day for some time. The most that can be said is that the novel, the play, and the magazine article revived that interest. A fictionalised treatment of the event is, in my view, as much in the public domain as would be a watercolour of the assassination of a public official. It seems to me irrelevant to talk of any right of privacy in this context. Here a private person is catapulted into the news by events over which he had no control. He and his activities are then in the public domain as fully as the matters at issue in *New York Times Co. v. Sullivan*.... Such privacy as a person normally has ceased when his life has ceased to be private[18].

There are a number of facts about the Hill case that makes it a little difficult to grasp[19]:

a) The case involved privacy, not libel.
b) The Hills were private citizens who involuntarily became subjects of public interest.
c) The case was originally tried before the New York Times case was decided.

d) The Hills' grievances were not easy to
    perceive in the case, as the story did not
    show them in an unfavourable light. If
    anything, part of the inaccuracies
    complained of in the story was that it
    stressed the Hills' "heroism in crisis".

Harry Kalven, Jr. has in fact suggested that
whatever "harm the story inflicted was not
because of the falsity but because it once again
exposed the Hills to the gaze of a national public."[20] In other words, the story tried to throw
them back to the status of 'involuntary public
figures', to which they had retreated.

Issues could be taken with some of the dicta
in the judgment especially the opinion of Justice Douglas quoted above. For instance it is
arguable whether the availability of information in the public domain necessarily makes
the information to be of public interest, and
whether Hill, who was forced by circumstances into being a 'public figure', could still
be treated as such after he had clearly expressed he was retreating to his life as a 'private citizen' and had discouraged all efforts to
keep himself and the family in the spotlight.
More troubling with this ruling is a denial of a
right of privacy to private individuals, who by
circumstances beyond their control, are thrust
into the eyes of the public. While freedom of
the press is necessary and should be cherished,
is it not also equally important that the dignity

of the individual, who is the foundational block of the democratic process, (which free speech is supposed to enhance), is also protected against the tyranny of the press?

Monitor Patriot v Roy[21]

On September 10, 1960, three days before the New Hampshire Democratic Party's primary election of candidates for the United States Senate, the *Concord Monitor*, a daily newspaper in Concord, New Hampshire, published a syndicated 'D.C. Merry-Go-Round' column discussing the forthcoming election. The column spoke of political manoeuvring in the primary campaign, referred to the criminal records of several of the candidates, and described Alphonse Roy, one of the candidates, as a 'former small-time bootlegger'

Roy, who was defeated in the election, sued the *Monitor Patriot Co.* and the North American Newspaper Alliance (NANA), the distributor of the column, for libel. The judge instructed the jury that Roy, as a candidate for Senate, was a "public official", (a characterisation which was not challenged,) and that the *New York Times v Sullivan* rule requiring a demonstration that the article was false and had been published "with knowledge of its falsity or with reckless disregard of whether it was false or true," applied as long as the libel concerned "official", as opposed to "private", conduct. On the characterisation of Roy as a 'public official', the Court held that "it might be preferable to categorize a candidate as a 'public figure', if for no other reason than to avoid straining the common meaning of words[22]".

The jury was also instructed that, if it found the libel to be in the "public sector", it had to bring in a verdict for the distributor, as there was no evidence that it had engaged in knowing or reckless falsehood, but that it had to decide on the "preponderance of the evidence" whether the newspaper was liable. This private-public distinction was elaborated as follows: "Is it more probable than otherwise that the publication that the plaintiff was a former small-time bootlegger was a public affair on a par with official conduct of public officials?"[23] The trial judge went on:

> "As a candidate for the United State Senate, the plaintiff was within the public official concept, and a candidate must surrender to public scrutiny and discussion so must his private character as it affects his fitness for office. That is, anything which might touch on Alphonse Roy's fitness for the office of United States Senator would come within the concept of official conduct. If it would not touch upon or be relevant to his fitness for the office for which he was a candidate but was rather a bringing forward of the plaintiff's long forgotten misconduct in

which the public had no interest, then it would be a private matter in the private sector.'[24]

If the alleged libel was in the "private sector", there were two defences: (1) "justification", if the article was true and published on a "lawful occasion", and (2) "conditional privilege," if the article was false, but if the publication was "on a lawful occasion, in good faith, for a justifiable purpose, and with a belief founded on reasonable grounds of the truth of the matter published. The jury in this case returned verdicts against both the newspaper and NANA. It most probably concluded that the bootlegger charge was in the 'private sector', since it had been instructed that unless it so found it could not impose liability on NANA. It is possible that having made this determination, it then concluded that the charge was true but 'unjustified'—that is, that it had been published without a 'lawful occasion.

The jury returned a verdict against both the newspaper and the distributor of the column. The State Supreme Court affirmed, holding that the jury properly considered whether the alleged libel was "relevant" to Roy's fitness for office.

The Court reformulated the 'official conduct' rule of New York Times in terms of 'anything which might touch on an official's fitness for office' to apply it to Roy as a candidate for public office, arguing that the principal activity of a candidate for political office in the US system was, so to speak, to put before the voters every conceivable aspect of his public and private life that he thinks may lead the electorate to gain a good impression of him. The Court gave example with a candidate who seeks to further his political career through the prominent display of his wife and children (selling himself to the electorate as a good family man), and held that such a candidate can hardly argue that his qualities as a husband or father remain of 'purely private' concern. Similarly a candidate who vaunts his spotless record and sterling integrity cannot convincingly cry 'foul!' when an opponent or an industrious reporter attempts to demonstrate the contrary. The Court further held:

> The clash of reputations is the staple of election campaigns, and damage to reputation is, of course, the essence of libel. But whether there remains some exiguous area of defamation against which a candidate may have full recourse is a question we need not decide in this case.[25]

The judgment was reversed and remanded in what we feel are strong grounds. From a 'public interest' perspective, we agree that a candidate for a political office is putting both his character and record to the electorate and as such should not complain, if the press brings up unfavourable stories about him that will aid the electorate in making their choice. The public is clearly interested in knowing all the information about a candidate, including unfavourable ones, to enable them make an informed choice, since the fact of campaigning for a public office implies selling one's self to the electorate. The proviso here should be that any of such unfavourable stories (and even favourable ones) should be substantially true, and should be written in adherence to the standards of responsible journalism. If a candidate enjoys favourable press coverage from a section of the media, (the slant of such stories could indeed mislead some of the electorate into voting for him), he should not complain if another section of the press feels obliged to 'put the record straight' about him by unearthing unfavourable stories about him, no matter how remote in time. Provided such unfavourable stories are true or substantially true, and that the standards of responsible journalism are followed, it will then be up to the electorate to weigh the favourable and unfavourable stories about the candidate and decide if he is indeed the right person for the office he seeks.

References

[1]   Chaplinsky   v   New   Hampshire   315   US 568n[1942]

2   The US Supreme Court in Paul v Davis 424 US
    693 [1976] held that reputation alone was not a
    'liberty' or 'property' interest protected by the
    Fourteenth Amendment.

3   Eric Barendt, Op Cit, p. 205

4   M.B. Nimmer (1968) "The Right to Speak from
    Times to *Time*: First Amendment Theory Applied
    to Libel and Misapplied to Privacy" 56 *Califor-
    nia Law Review*

5   *New York Times Co. v. Sullivan,* 376 U.S. 254
    [1964]

6   *Brown v. Board of Education of Topeka,* 347
    U.S. 483[1954]

7   *Plessy v. Ferguson,* 163 U.S. 537 [1896]

8   *Whitney v. California,* 274 U. S. 357

9   Ibid [at S. 375-376]

10 Lee C. Bollinger (1991) "End of New York Ti-
    mes v Sullivan: Reflections on Mason v New
    Yorker Magazine" *Sup Ct. Rev* 1

11 *Curtis Publishing Co. v. Butts,* 388 U.S. 130
    [1967]

12 Ibid [pp130-131]

13 Ibid, [Pp. 148, 152-154].

14 Ibid [p. 155]

15 Ibid [p. 156-158]

16 Ibid [at p.163]

17 *Time, Inc v Hill* 385 U.S. 374 [1967]

18 Ibid [at p. 401]

19 See Harry Kalven, Jr. [1967] "The Reasonable Man and the First Amendment: Hill, Butts and Walker", Sup. *Ct. Rev* 267, (p. 272)

20 Ibid [at pp272-273]

21 *Monitor Patriot Co. v. Roy*, 401 U.S. 265 (1971)

22 Ibid [at p.271]

23 Ibid [at pp268-269]

24 Ibid [at p.269]

25 Ibid [at 275]

Chapter 5

FREE SPEECH, PROTECTION OF REPUTATION, AND PUBLIC INTEREST DEFENCE IN ENGLISH LAW OF DEFAMATION: CASE LAW

Introduction

In Britain, but less so in the USA, there is an almost supreme belief in the power of words to wound and destroy one's reputation such that often any critical reference to a prominent person risks bringing forth a "pompously threatening solicitor's letter but in America, defamatory words scattered on the raging sea of communication are usually ignored."[1] Hence London is regarded as the defamation capital of the world, with American journalists nicknaming it "a town named Sue".[2] But how is free speech interests balanced with the need to protect reputation in English defamation law? How is public interest defence construed? To answer these questions we will look at some case law.

Derbyshire County Council v Times Newspapers Ltd and Others[3]

On 17 and 24 September 1989, the *Sunday Times* published two articles concerning share deals involving the superannuation fund of the Derbyshire County Council, a local authority. The articles in the issue of 17 September were headed 'Revealed: Socialist tycoon's deals with a Labour chief' and 'Bizarre deals of a council leader and the media tycoon'; that in the issue of 24 September was headed 'Council share deals under scrutiny'. The council leader was Mr David Melvyn Bookbinder; the 'media tycoon' was Mr Owen Oyston. The articles questioned the propriety of certain investments made by the council of moneys in its superannuation fund, with Mr Bookbinder as the prime mover, in three deals with Mr Oyston or companies controlled by him.

The Council sued, arguing that the publications had injured its credit and reputation and had brought it into public scandal, odium and contempt, leading it to suffer loss and damage[4]. There was a preliminary issue of whether the claimant had a cause of action against the defendants. The claimant argued that in exercising its powers and carrying out its functions as a county council, it has a reputation that is distinct from that of its individual members or officers.

Prior to this case there were only two reported cases in which a local authority had sued for libel. The first is *Manchester Corporation v Williams* [1891] 1 QB 94, 63 LT 805. In this case the defendant had written a letter to a newspaper alleging bribery and corruption in the council. A Divisional Court held that the statement of claim disclosed no cause of action, and that a corporation may sue for a libel affecting property but not for one merely affecting personal reputation.

The second case involving proceedings by a local authority is *Bognor Regis Urban District Council v Campion* [1972] 2 QB 169. In this case the council sued Mr Campion, who had distributed a leaflet savagely attacking the council at a meeting of ratepayers' association. At the trial Mr Campion conducted his own case without the assistance of solicitors or counsel. Browne J found in favour of the council and awarded it damages of GBP2, 000. At p173, He reasoned:

> "Just as a trading company has a trading reputation which it is entitled to protect by bringing an action for defamation, so in my view the plaintiffs as a local government corporation have a 'governing' reputation which they are equally entitled to protect in the same way--of course, bearing in mind the vital distinction between defamation of the corporation as such and defamation of its individual officers or members[5].

In the Derbyshire case, the judge held that a local authority could sue for libel in respect of its governmental and administrative functions, and dismissed the defendants' application to strike out the statement of claim. The Court of Appeal however held that the claimant could not bring the action for libel. On appeal by the claimant, the judge held that since it was of the highest public importance that a democratically elected governmental body should be open to uninhibited public criticism, and since the threat of civil actions for defamation would place an undesirable fetter on the freedom to express such criticism, it would be contrary to the public interest for institutions of central or local government to have any right at common law to maintain an action for damages for defamation. The case was consequently struck out.

The notion of public interest adopted here is the need to hold public officials accountable, and the democracy argument, used to justify free speech as we discussed earlier. The reasoning in the decision is that being a government body, in which all citizens and residents are stakeholders, it would be of paramount importance for such a body to be open to uninhibited public criticism. The Court's belief was that the fundamental principle of freedom of speech was involved in the case, and that individuals should enjoy absolute privilege to criticise inefficient or corrupt government without fear of civil and criminal prosecution. Here the decision rightly protects the free speech rights of the individual as the foundational block of this democratic process as well as the watchdog role of the press in a democracy.

It is interesting to note the influence of the *New York Times v Sullivan* case, which was approvingly cited in the case. It is also instructive that the Court took into consideration Art 10 of the European Convention on Human Rights even thought it had not been then formally incorporated into English laws. In fact, Barendt attributed part of the reasons for the outcome in the case to the European Convention on Human rights, arguing:

> The Court of Appeal ruling is remarkable not only for its result, but also because of the bold use by the court of the Convention to develop a point of common law, which (in its view) was far from clear, namely the capacity of public authorities to sue for libel[6].

While the council is denied a right to bring libel proceedings, it was still allowed, it if chose, to bring proceedings with respect to its reputation through action for malicious falsehood. The Court of Appeal reasoned that such "protection should be seen as all that is necessary in a democratic society for the protection of reputation and rights of a local government authority".[7]

Reynolds v Times Newspapers Ltd[8]

The events, which gave rise to these proceedings, took place during a political crisis in Dublin in November 1994. The crisis culminated in the resignation of Mr. Reynolds as Taoiseach (prime minister) of Ireland and leader of the Fianna Fáil party. The reasons for Mr. Reynolds' resignation were clearly of public significance and interest in the United Kingdom primarily because of his personal identification with the Northern Ireland peace process as one of the chief architects of that process.

Mr Reynolds announced his resignation from the Dáil (the House of Representatives) of the Irish Parliament on Thursday, 17 November 1994. The following Sunday, 20 November, the *Sunday Times* published in its British mainland edition an article entitled 'Goodbye gombeen man.' The article was the lead item in its world news section and occupied most of one page. It was sub-headed 'Why a fib too far proved fatal for the political career of Ireland's peacemaker and Mr. Fixit'. On the same day, the Irish edition of the *Sunday Times* contained a three page article headed 'House of Cards' concerning the fall of the Government. This article differed in a number of respects from the British mainland edition.

Mr. Reynolds took strong exception to the article in the British mainland edition. In the libel proceedings, which followed, Mr. Reynolds pleaded that the sting of the article was that he had deliberately and dishonestly misled the Dáil on Tuesday, 15 November 1994 by suppressing vital information. Further, that he had deliberately and dishonestly misled his coalition cabinet colleagues, especially Mr. Spring, the Tanaiste (deputy prime minister) and minister for foreign affairs, by withholding this information and had lied to them about when the information had come into his possession. The author of the article was Mr. Ruddock, the newspaper's Irish editor. Times Newspapers Ltd. was the publisher of the newspaper, and Mr. Witherow was the editor. They were defendants in the proceedings. By instituting and prosecuting the libel action Mr. Reynolds had waived his immunity under the Irish constitution in respect of proceedings in the Dáil.

The House of Lords rejected arguments by the *Times Newspapers* that because Reynolds was a powerful political figure, the occasion of publication was necessarily privileged. It however held that privilege could attach to any communication, whether or not about politics, so long as it concerned a matter of serious public interest. It established that the publication of information which the public has a "right to know", may, regardless of the fact that it could later turn out to be false, be made on an occasion of privilege – though this privilege would be lost if it is proved that the publication was actuated by malice - whether legal (i.e. dishonesty or recklessness towards the truth) or actual (i.e. spite or desire for profit). A newspaper was therefore entitled to put into the public domain information, which has been reasonably checked and sourced as part of a discussion of matters of serious public interest.

From a free speech perspective, it is interesting to note that journalists will not lose this privilege if they refuse to disclose the sources of their story. There are two inter-related conditions for the existence of this privilege: (a) that the newspaper has a "duty" to publish because the information appears important and credible and the claimant had been treated fairly and (2) the public have a legitimate (rather than a prurient or passing interest) in receiving it.

Lord Nicols devised ten non-exhaustive factors, which must be taken into consideration in assessing whether the circumstances of publication warranted the protection of qualified privilege. These factors, which could also be called tests of responsible journalism, (and hence 'objective' grounds for assessing whether the press has sought to subordinate the individual to its whims) were:

1) The seriousness of the allegation
2) The nature of the information and the extent to which the subject matter is a matter of public concern
3) The source of the information – some informants have no direct knowledge of the subject matter
4) The status of the information – the allegation may already be in the public domain or a subject of investigation, which makes it to command respect
5) The steps taken to verify the information
6) The urgency of the matter – news is open and perishable commodity
7) Whether comment was sought by the claimant
8) Whether the article contained the gist of the claimant's side of the story
9) The tone of the article
10) The circumstances of publication, including the timing.

It is instructive to note that the *Sunday Times* lost the case because it was deemed to have behaved irresponsibly, omitting Reynolds's side of the story and unfairly sensationalising allegations that were never made in its Irish edition. In other words, it would seem as if the Reynolds' approach, with its 10 factors of what could also be a good way of 'measuring' malice, sought not to allow the fear of libel to chill discussions in matters of public interest, but at the same time took extra care to ensure that individuals are not subordinated to the whims of the press in the

name of public interest. This is demonstrated
by its rejection of a plea by the *Sunday Times*
to develop 'political information' as a new
subject matter category of qualified privilege,
whatever the circumstance. Lord Nicols argued
that to develop such

> " ...would not provide adequate safeguard for
> reputation. Moreover it would be unsound in
> principle to distinguish political discussion
> from discussion of other matters of serious
> concern"[9].

In Bonnick *v Morris*, Lord Nichols reprised
the 'deal' between the media and the judiciary
under the Reynolds's approach:

> 'Stated shortly the *Reynolds* privilege is con-
> cerned to provide a proper degree of protection
> for responsible journalism when reporting mat-
> ters of public concern. Responsible journalism
> is the point at which a fair balance is held be-
> tween freedom of expression on matters of pub-
> lic concern and the reputations of individuals.
> Maintenance of this standard is in the public in-
> terest and in the interests of those whose repu-
> tations are involved. It can be regarded as the
> price journalists pay in return for the privilege.
> If they are to have the benefit of the privilege
> journalists must exercise due professional skill
> and care.'[10]

The decision in Reynolds however is not
without its critics. Loveland has for instance

noted that its ten-point "right to know" test appeared to have

> "...transferred decision making power on those factual issues from the jury to judge and also *de facto* transferred the burden of proof on quite important questions from the claimant to the defendant It was primarily because of disquiet with these consequences that the *Reynolds* principle was promptly rejected by the New Zealand Court of Appeal in *Lange v Atkinson*. In a quite uncomplicated fashion, *Lange* extended qualified privilege to press coverage of the political activities of politicians and left matters pertaining to the way in which the story was produced and published for the jury to consider in the malice stage of the qualified privilege inquiry[11].

George Galloway v Telegraph Group Ltd[12]

The claimant George Galloway was a well-known Member of Parliament. He had sued the *Daily Telegraph* for damages for libel on the ground that he was defamed in the paper's editions of April 22 and 23, 2003. The first article complained of was published on April 22, 2003, which was just over a month after the invasion of Iraq by coalition forces and at a time when British and American troops were still heavily engaged in fighting. The articles were based on documents found by the paper's reporter in Baghdad ("the Baghdad documents"). On April 21, the day before publication, an employee of the *Daily Telegraph* telephoned the claimant and asked him for his reaction to a number of points arising out of the documents, which had been found in Baghdad.

There were four articles complained of in the issue of April 22. The first was on the front page, under the heading: "Galloway was in Saddam's pay, say secret Iraqi documents." Underneath appeared three bullet point subheadings as follows: "Labour MP 'received at least £375,000 a year'"; "Cash came from oil for food programme"; and "Papers could have been forged, he says". The fourth article complained of in the issue of April 22 consisted of a leader headed "Saddam's little helper" which was the only leader published in the *Daily Telegraph* that day.

Eady J. tried the case without a jury. He handed down judgment on December 2, 2004. He held that the articles complained of were seriously defamatory of the claimant and said the articles had conveyed the following meanings, among others, to reasonable and fairminded readers: that the claimant had been in the pay of Saddam Hussein, secretly receiving sums of money of about £375,000 a year; that he had diverted monies from the oil-for-food programme, thus depriving the Iraqi people, whose interests he had claimed to represent, of food and medicines; that what the claimant had done was tantamount to treason; and that he had probably used the Mariam Appeal as a front for personal enrichment.

The case generated a lot of media interest, in part because Mr Galloway had been a strident critic of the Iraq war, who was perhaps best known for his vigorous campaign to overturn the economic sanctions against Iraq in the 1990s and early 2000s and to avert the 2003 invasion of that country. He had visited Iraq in1994 and 2002 and was received by the Iraqi leader Saddam Hussein.

There was no doubt that the issue was of great public interest. But for the proceedings, the battleground was whether the *Daily Telegraph* could rely on these documents to claim a defence of qualified privilege. The answer was that under the Reynolds test for qualified privilege they could, but only insofar as their comment on the documents was fair. As we noted earlier, fair comment, means that the comments must be based on opinions expressed on available facts. Statements of facts presented by the paper, even if presented as opinions, must be justified (see *Telnikoff v Masutevich* discussed earlier).

In its appeal, the *Daily Telegraph* claimed that Mr Justice Eady had not differentiated between fact and comment and suggested that because the judge did not like the comment, the paper was unfairly being punished for exposing the facts. Delivering the judgment of the Appeal Court, Sir Anthony Clarke MR upheld the decision of the High Court on all counts.

The Court accepted that the allegations against Mr Galloway were potentially capable of being reported in a way, which would be protected by qualified privilege. It held that

> "...if the documents had been published without comment or serious allegations of fact Mr Galloway could have no complaint since, in so far as they contained statements or allegations of fact it was in the public interest for the Telegraph to publish them, at any rate after giving Mr Galloway a fair opportunity to respond to them"[13].

The Court also held that if the *Daily Telegraph* had investigated the veracity of the documents and their claims, it would perhaps have forced the paper to publish a far less sensational article. Such a course of action, it reasoned, would also perhaps have taken the paper longer to publish the articles. But the gain, had the paper followed that course of action, from a protection of reputation perspective, is that it would clearly. Had forced it to be less sensational in its reporting. One of the lessons from the ruling may well be that if inflammatory documents fall into the hands of a media organisation, they would be best advised to bear in mind Reynolds ten-point test of

responsible journalism before publishing if
they wish to rely upon a Reynolds defence if
they are sued for libel.

It is remarkable that the Court of Appeal
agreed with Eady J that the *Daily Telegraph*
was alleging guilt and adopting the allegations
in the documents as its own, rather than calling
for an investigation into the claims or reporting
the allegations. Worse still, the Court agreed
with Eady J that the *Daily Telegraph* had em-
bellished the allegations in the Baghdad documents. For instance while the documents only
appeared to suggest that the Mariam Appeal
and Mr Galloway's campaigning had been
funded by Oil For Food money, the paper had
gone beyond that and suggested that Mr
Galloway was gaining personally from the alleged payments.

The *Daily Telegraph* was also held not to
have put the whole of the allegations to Mr
Galloway, and to have failed to put his side of
the case in sufficient detail. Notably, the tran-
script of the reporter's conversation with Mr
Galloway showed that the allegation that Mr
Galloway had received money for his personal
benefit had not been put to him. Since this was
a very serious allegation, responsible journalism demanded that it should be put to him.
Similarly the paper appeared unconvinced by
Mr Galloway's denials of the other allegations
against him, describing his denials as "bluster"

and an attempt to "explain away" the allegations. The Court therefore held that the paper's efforts to get Mr Galloway's side of the story was insufficient and could not be counted as putting Mr Galloway's side of the case.

Eady J also made something of the fact that the Telegraph could have printed the story at any time, that there was really no urgency to print the story at the time it did, and that the paper could have taken its time to investigate the claims and obtain proper comments. He maintained that although news is a perishable commodity, in these circumstances there was no need to rush into print especially as the documents were not in any danger of being lost as they had been scanned and sent electronically to London.

One of the lessons from the Galloway case is that even controversial politicians regarded by the government of the day as an irritant, has a reputation to protect, and rightly so. Another lesson is that journalists should take care when writing a controversial story in order to avoid over-egging the pudding. They should publish both sides of such a story and tailor the story they write to the defence they intend to employ, if they are threatened with libel.

The acceptance by the Court of Appeal that a privileged article could have been written, and the guidance as to how to do it, should be a good lesson for publishers, who in a bid to make a scoop, or level up with a critic of the war which it supported, unwittingly substituted its own interest for the public interest. The decision has not changed the law - but it has again demonstrated best practice and the importance of writing a controversial article with a defence in mind. Above all it is worth noting the sentiments expressed in the judgment, in defence of reputation, especially of people who have prominently taken a position against a war in which the defendant newspaper had supported. Galloway's counsel, Richard Rampton QC in fact reportedly told the Appeal Court judges that their decision was "one of the most unequivocally emphatic judgments he had ever come across in this field of law."[14] In an article aptly entitled: "What price irresponsible journalism? Reflections on the Galloway litigation", Duncan Bloy wrote of the judgment in the Galloway case:

> It surely is naïve to suggest that those making the editorial decisions at the *Telegraph* were unaware of the ten non-exhaustive factors identified by Lord Nichols as equating to 'responsible journalism'. Indeed, it cannot be doubted that the House of Lords' decision was anything other than 'media friendly'.[15]

Yes, the Reynolds' approach is media friendly but as we can also see in the Galloway case, its checklist against irresponsible journalism, could also be good hurdles aimed at protecting people's reputation, or to prevent giving the press a blank cheque.

References

1   Geoffrey Robertson and Andrew Nicol Op Cit p.72

2   Ibid p.71

3   *Derbyshire County Council v Times Newspapers Ltd and Others]* W.L.R. 28 *[1992]*

4   Ibid [at 32]

5   Ibid [at 40]

6   Eric Barendt [1992] "Case Comment: Government, Libel and Freedom of Speech", *Public Law* (Autumn, p.360

7   *Derbyshire County Council v Times Newspapers Ltd and Others* W.L.R. 28*[1992]* [at 55 F (iii)]

8   *Reynolds v Times Newspapers Ltd [2001] 2.A.C.*

9   Ibid [at 204]

10 *Bonnick v Morris* UKPC 31[2003] [at 23].

11 Ian Loveland (2003) "The ongoing evolution of Reynolds privilege in domestic libel law" in *Entertainment Law Review,* 14 (7) p179

12 *George Galloway v Telegraph Group Ltd* E.M.L.R. 11[2006]

13 Ibid [p244 at 48]

14 Cited in Duncan Bloy [2006]: "What price irresponsible journalism? Reflections on the Galloway litigation" *Comms. L.* 2006, 11(1), p.13

15 Ibid [at p. 13]

Chapter 6

CONCLUSIONS

We have discussed free speech and its rationale, pointing out that it is never absolute in any jurisdiction because of the need to balance it with other competing values such as the need to protect reputation. We also discussed the protection of reputation and defamation, including distinguishing between libel, slander and malicious falsehood. We equally discussed the notion of 'public interest', which is often used by the media to justify its attack on reputation, pointing out some of the definitional problems with the concept. Within that notion we discussed 'public figures' and 'public officials' – two categories of people who are the media's favourite whipping boys, and whose activities generate a lot of interests that the media often define as being in the 'public interest'. We also discussed the notion of 'malice', which is central to any public interest defence, because any proof of malice, often means that the public interest defence crumbles.

With a focus on the balancing act between free speech and the need to protect 'public interest' and people's reputation, we examined some cases in the USA and the UK. In the

USA we examined four cases - *New York Times v Sullivan* (involving a public official), *Curtis Publishing Co. v. Butts* (involving a public figure), *Time Inc v Hill* (involving a private individual who was transformed into a public figure against his will), *and Monitor Patriot v Roy* (involving a candidate for a political office). In the UK we examined *Derbyshire County Council v Times Newspapers Ltd. and Others* (involving a local authority, which sued for libel), *Reynolds v Times Newspapers Ltd* (involving a politician), *and George Galloway v Telegraph Group Ltd (*involving a controversial politician who was famous for opposing the Iraq war and the UN's sanctions against the country). We found for instance that in some of the cases such as *New York Times v Sullivan*, the notion of 'public interest' espoused by the US Supreme Court could be justified against the context of the case – in this instance the need to remove the 'chilling effect' on free speech occasioned by the threat of libel actions following the *Brown v Board of Education* case. We accept the notion of 'public interest' implied in the case despite the fact that the press could abuse the extremely high threshold set for proving 'actual malice' standard established in the case. In *George Galloway v Telegraph Group*, we argued that the press clearly engaged in irresponsible journalism, and substituted its interest for the 'public interest'. We questioned the decision in *Time Inc v Hill*, in which the Court ruled that it was in the public interest to publish a distorted story about a private individual who was transformed into a public figure against his wish, and who had clearly indicated that he did not wish to be in the limelight and desired the right to be left alone. We felt that in that case the Court went overboard by subordinating an individual's right to privacy to the public whim.

INDEX

A

A v B plc, 7, 14
Abrams v US, 2, 13
African Union, 39
Alabama, 50, 51, 53, 54, 55
Associated Press, 59, 60
Associated Press v Walker, 59, 60

B

Baghdad, 85, 89
Barendt, Eric, 4, 9, 10, 13, 14, 15, 73, 79, 92
BBC, 31
Bognor Regis Urban District Council v Campion, 77
Bollinger, Lee C, 14, 54, 73
Bonnick v Morris, 84, 92
Bookbinder, Melvyn, 76
bootlegger, 68, 69, 70
Brown v Board of Education of Topeka, 48, 73
Bryant, Paul, 55, 56
Burnett, George, 55, 56, 61, 62
Butts, Wally, 55, 56, 57, 59, 61, 62, 63, 74
Byrne v Deane, 22, 25

C

Campbell v Spottiswoode, 28, 44
certiorari, 56, 61
Chafee Jr, Zechariah, 8, 14

China, 49
City University, London, ix
civil rights movements, 54
claimant, 19, 20, 22, 23, 24, 31, 40, 41, 42, 43, 44, 52, 54, 76, 78, 82, 83, 85, 86
Code of Practice of the Press Complaints Commission, 38
Cold War, 50
colonialism, 49
Columbia Broadcasting System v Democratic National Committee, 10, 15
Communist countries, 49
Court of Appeal, 4, 22, 31, 33, 37, 78, 79, 85, 89, 90
Court of Appeals for the Fifth Circuit, 56
Crone, Tom, 17, 25, 29, 44
Curtis Publishing Co. v Butts, viii, 55, 73, 94
Curtis Publishing Company, 55

D

Dáil, 80, 81
Daily Telegraph, 31, 85, 86, 87, 88, 89
defamatory falsehood, 52, 57, 58
defendant, viii, 23, 31, 41, 42, 43, 51, 76, 85, 91

www.ingramcontent.com/pod-product-compliance
Lightning Source LLC
Chambersburg PA
CBHW021536260326
41914CB00001B/45